NEW AGE PIANO
WEDDING
COLLECTION

BEAUTIFUL WEDDING MUSIC FROM 13 NEW AGE ARTISTS

CONTENTS

Cover photo: Eric Naaman

ISBN 0-634-00578-2

7777 W. BLUEMOUND RD. P.O. BOX 13819 MILWAUKEE, WI 53213

Visit Hal Leonard Online at
www.halleonard.com

Angels Crossing

By TOM GRANT

Flowing, with a steady pulse

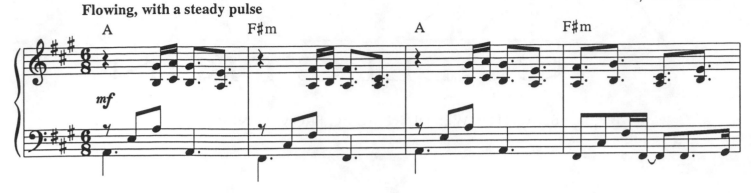

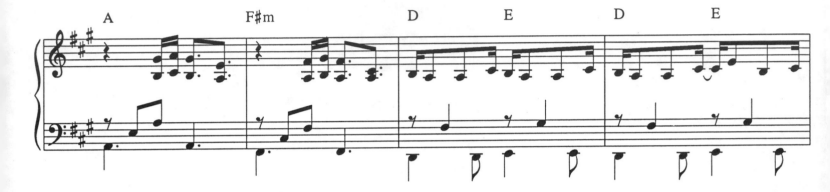

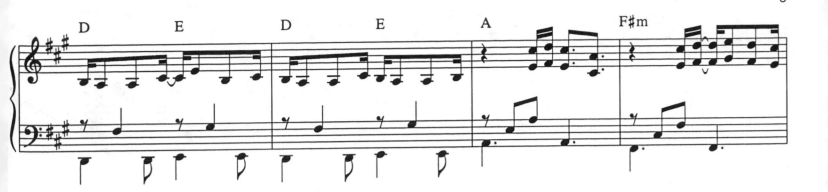

4

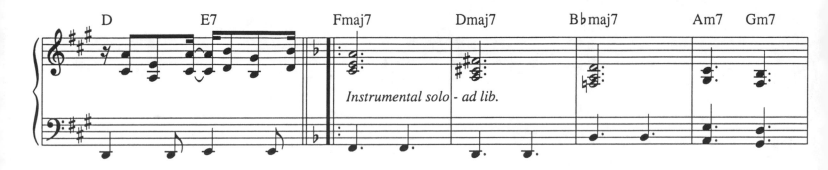

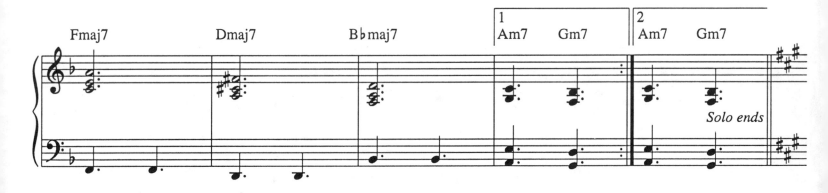

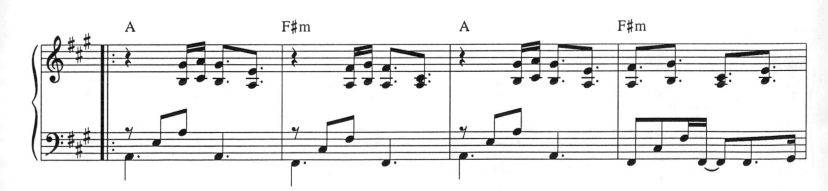

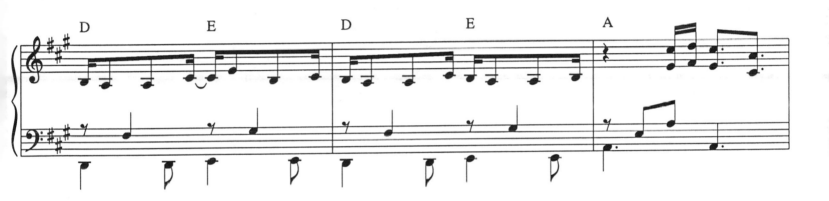

Repeat and Fade

Anthem of My Heart

Music by ROBIN SPIELBERG

Moderately slow

mf

with pedal

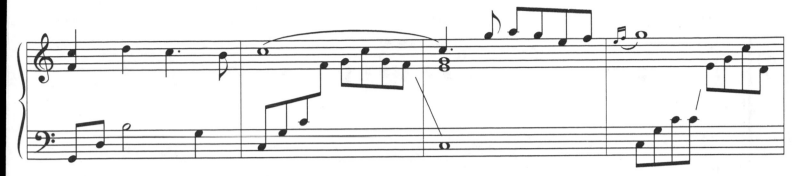

8

Gently

*Substitute small notes 2nd time.

Slightly slower

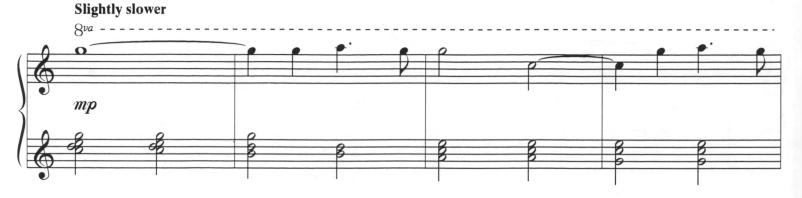

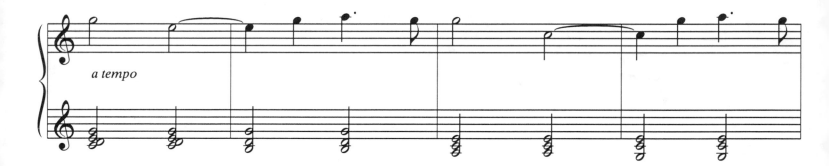

cresc.

Every Deep Dream

Composed and Arranged by
PHILIP AABERG

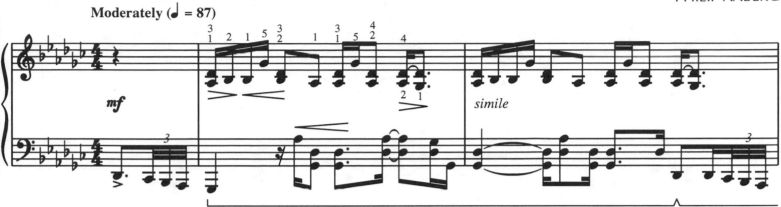

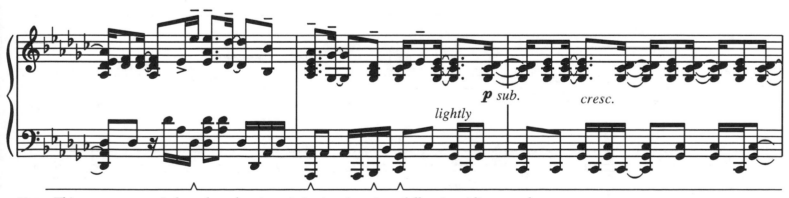

Note: This arrangement is based on the piano imitating American folk guitar idioms such as hammering-on. When performing, keep the 16th-note rhythm as steady as possible.

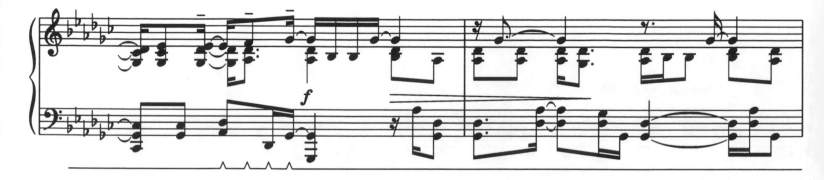

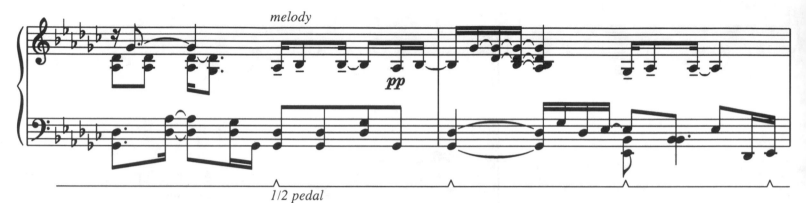

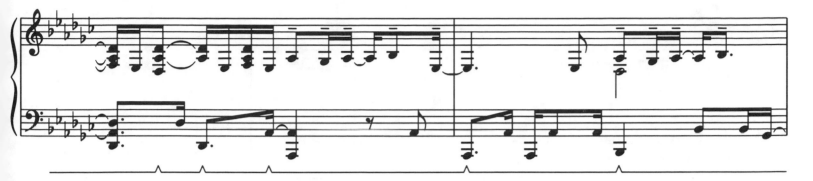

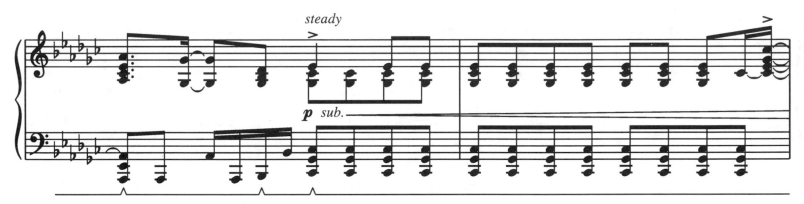

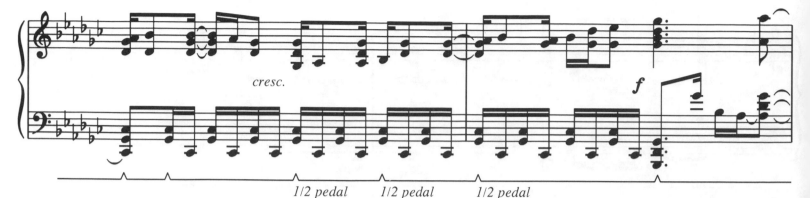

cresc.

f

1/2 pedal　　*1/2 pedal*　　*1/2 pedal*

4　　5　　5　　1

cresc.

Devotion

By LIZ STORY

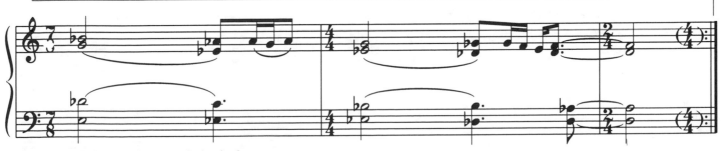

* 12/8 and 9/8 in this piece remain in *duple* meter
(the beat is subdivided by two).

From My Heart

By JIM CHAPPELL

Slowly

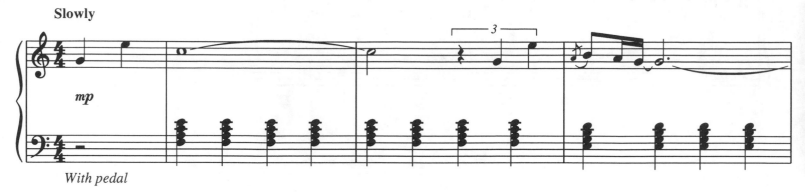

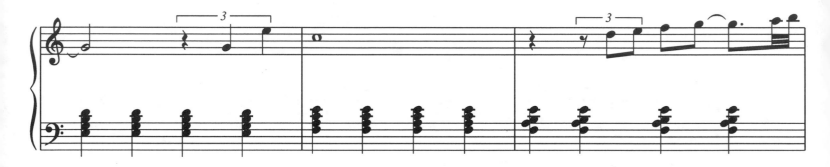

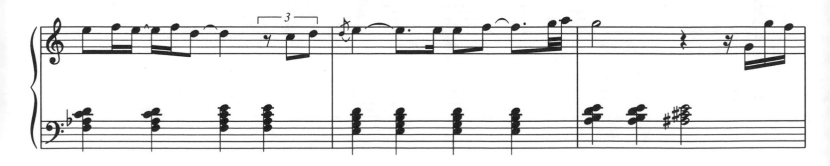

Improvisation repeats

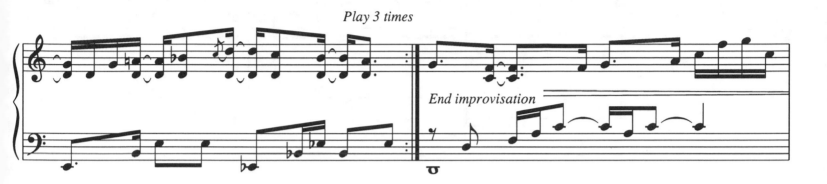

Play 3 times

End improvisation

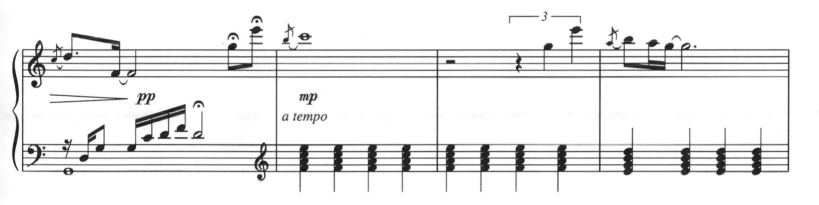

pp

mp

a tempo

3

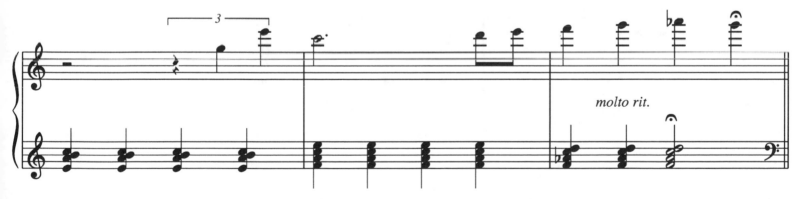

3

molto rit.

Repeat ad lib.

Improvise freely

Ped.   *

Heartsounds

By DAVID LANZ

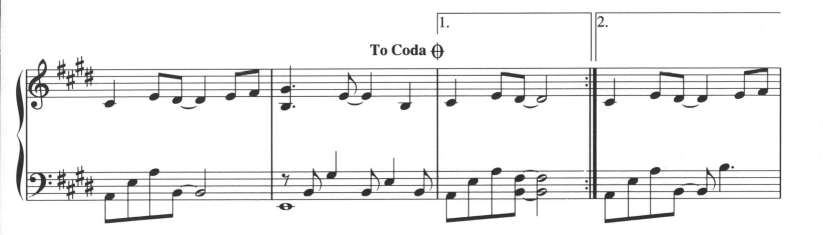

D.C. al Coda

CODA

The Key of Love

Music by JOHN TESH

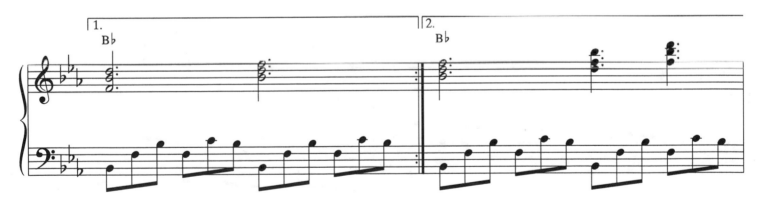

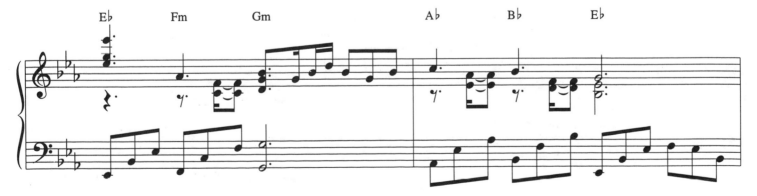

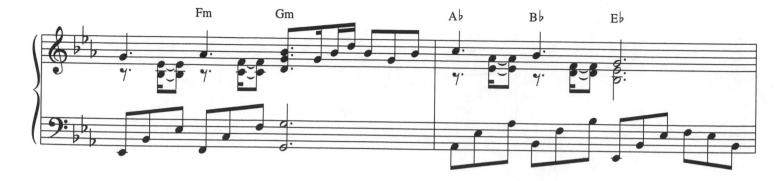

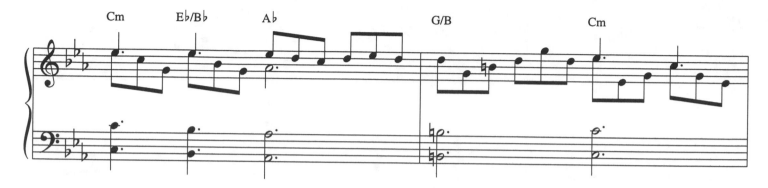

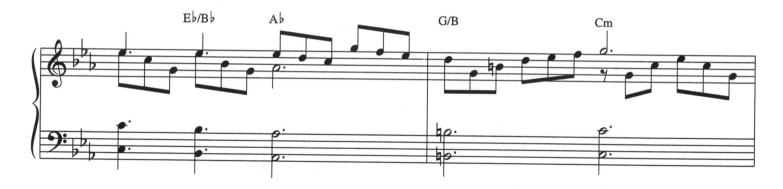

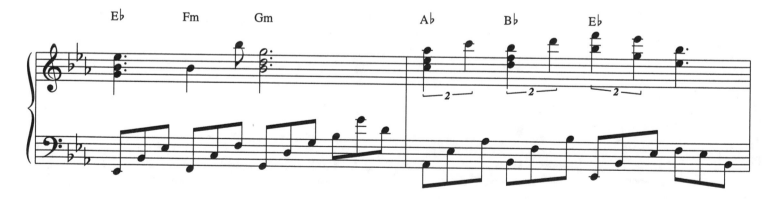

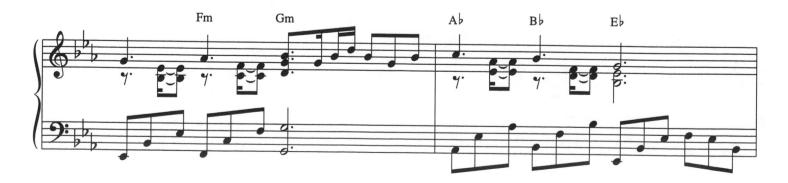

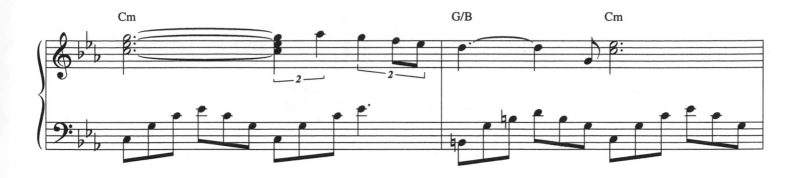

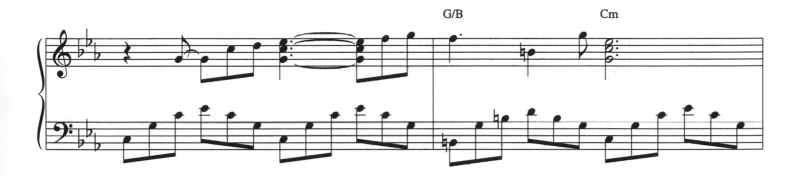

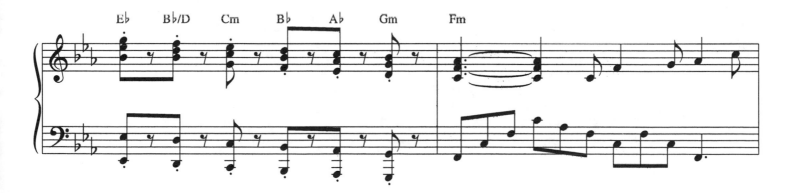

Pianoscapes

By MICHAEL JONES

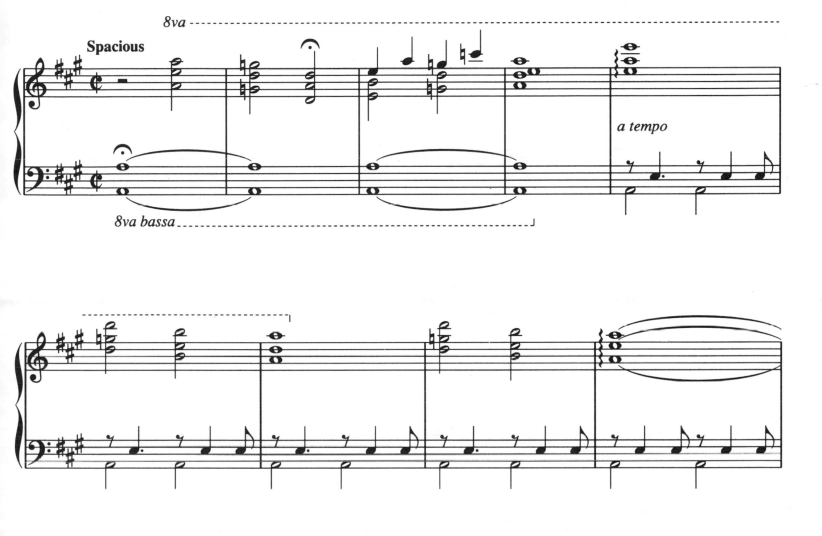

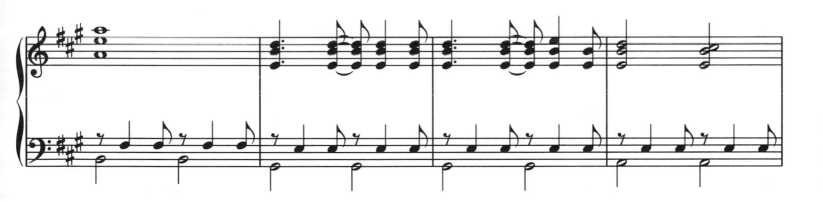

To Coda ⊕

Full, expressive

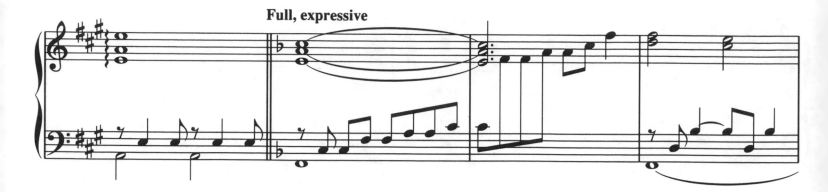

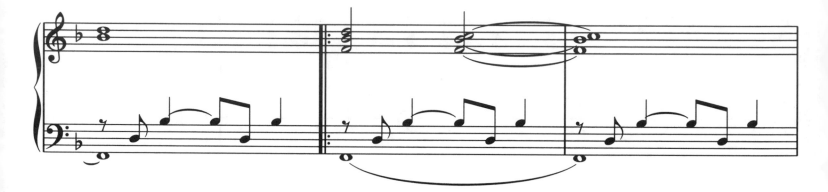

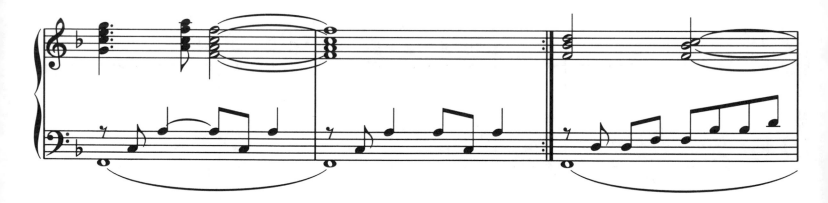

Playful
8va -

pp *slow cresc.*

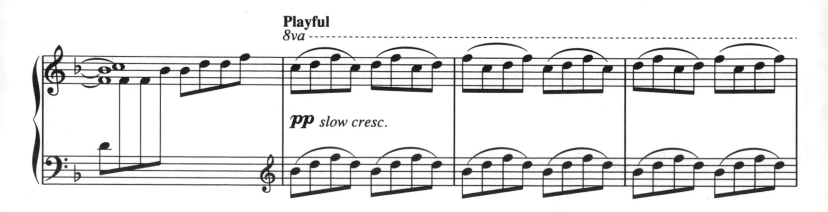

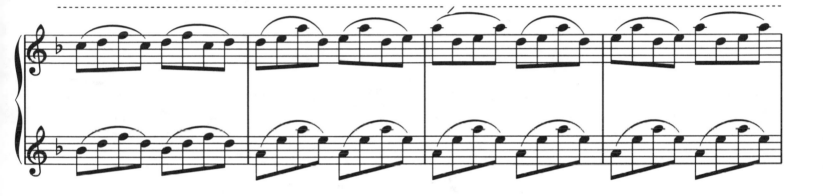

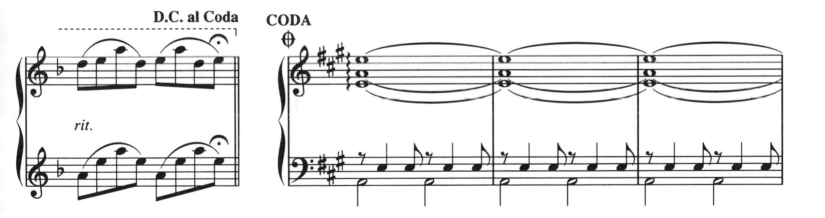

D.C. al Coda

CODA

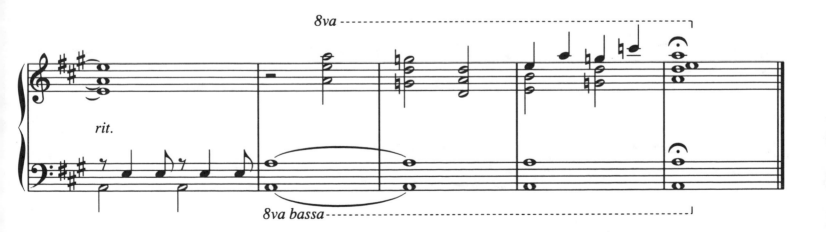

Part of My Heart

By JIM BRICKMAN

Moderately fast

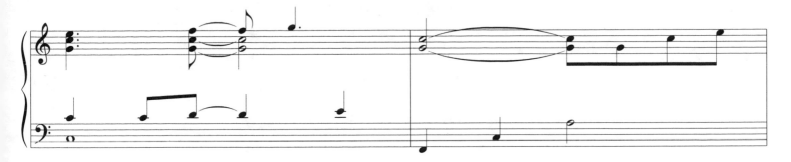

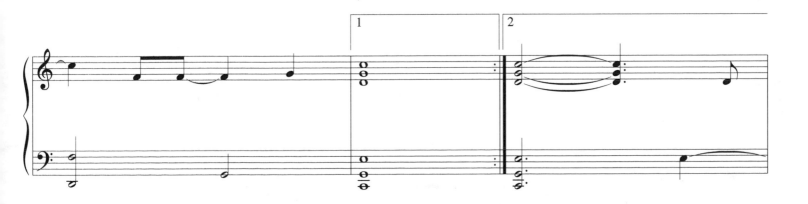

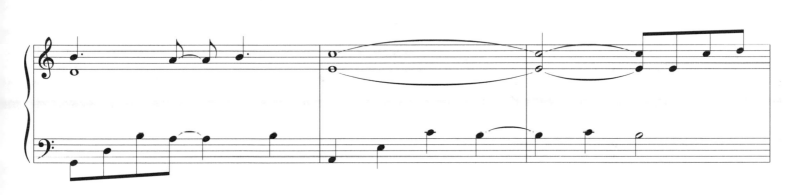

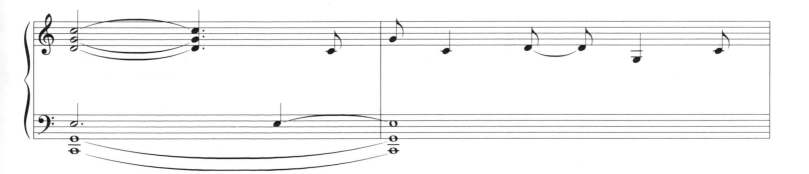

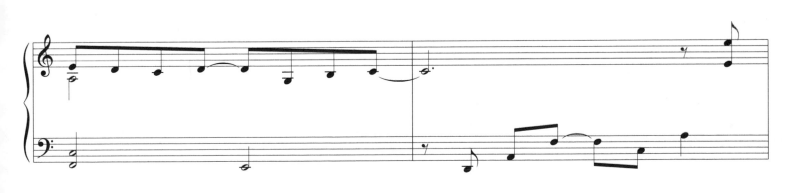

A Place Called Home

By SPENCER BREWER

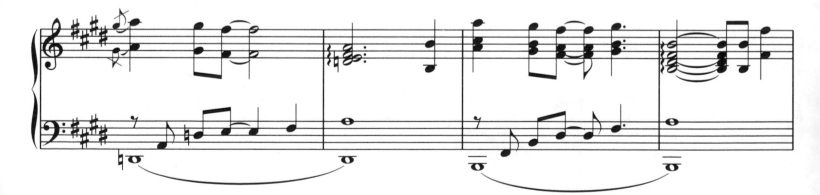

53

To Coda ⊕

D.S. al Coda

CODA

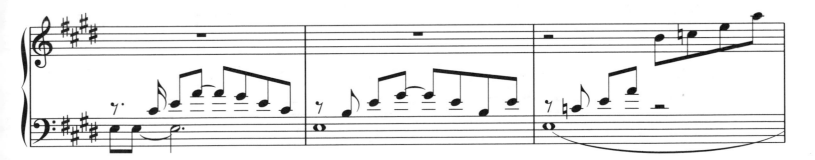

The Shape of Her Face

By MICHAEL WHALEN

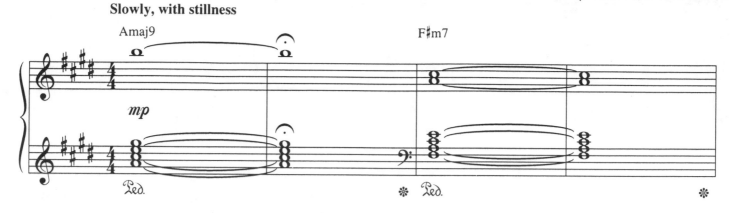

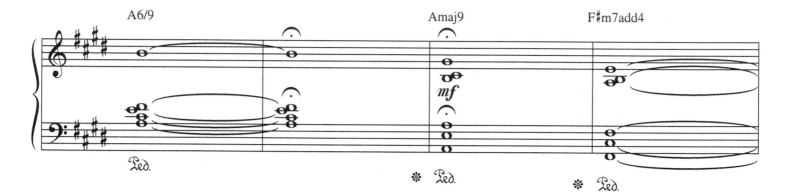

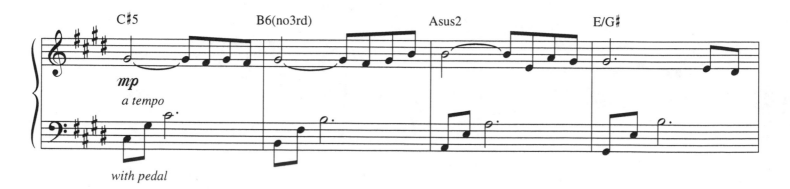

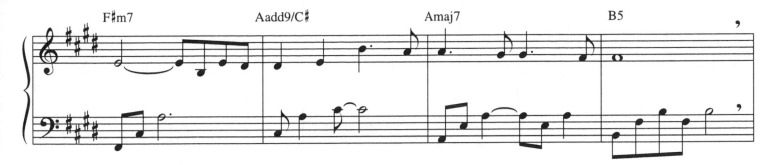

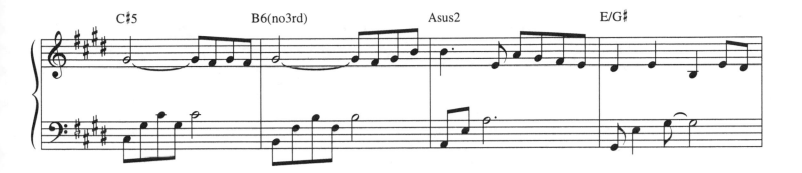

A little bigger, emotionally

Tempo I

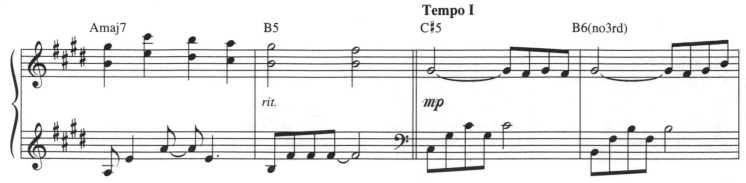

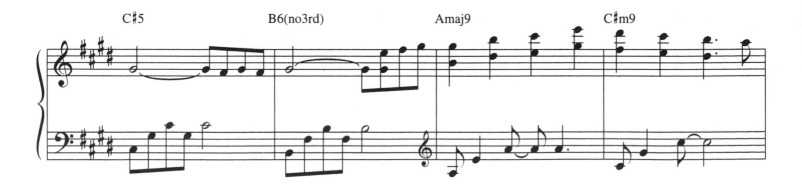

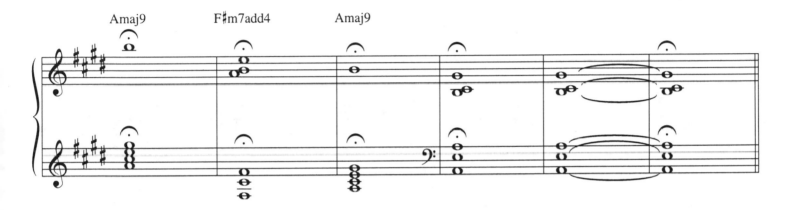

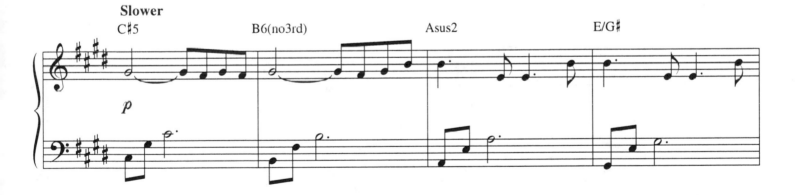

So Close

By WAYNE GRATZ

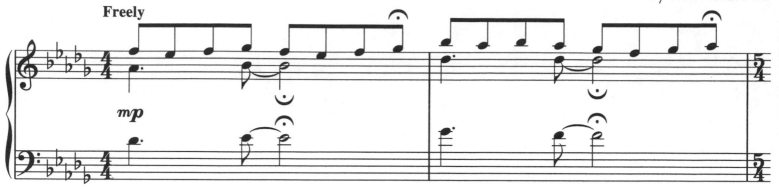

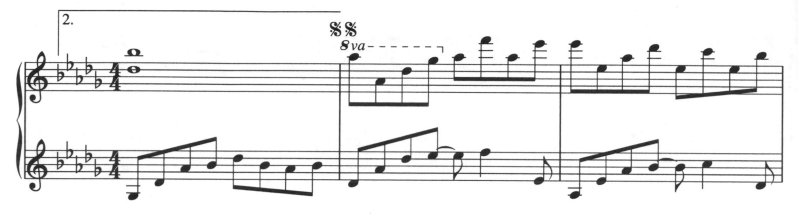

To Coda II ⊕ ⊕

D.S. al Coda

CODA

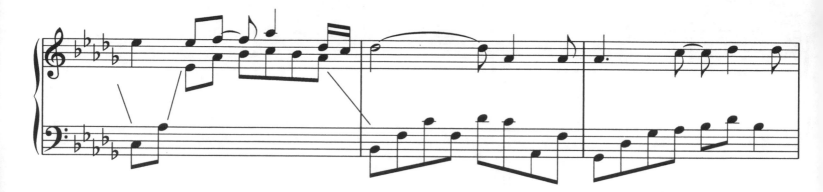

D.S.S. al Coda II

CODA II

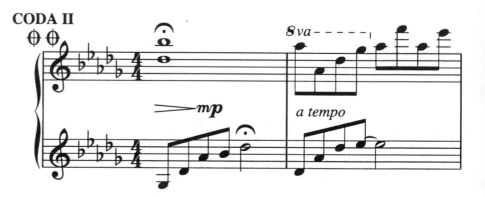

a tempo

Slower

molto rit.

8va bassa

Tender Ritual

By JIM CHAPPELL

Slowly and Expressively

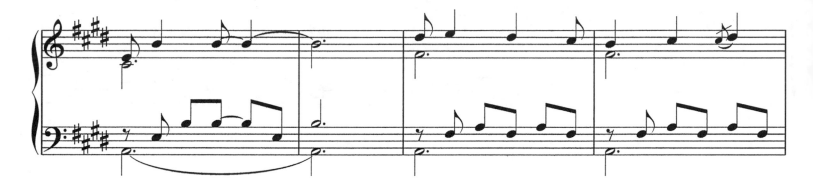

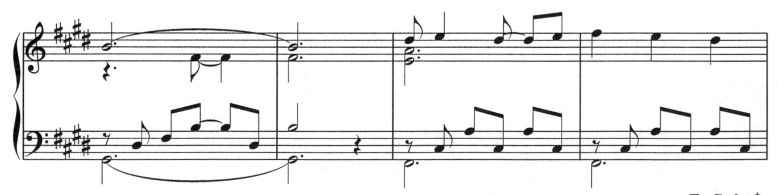

To Coda ⊕

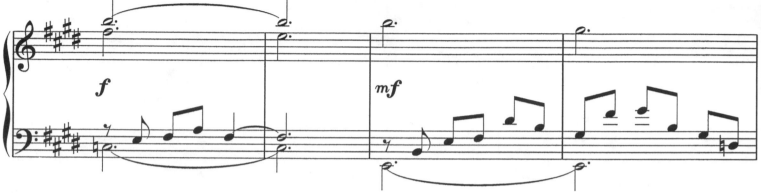

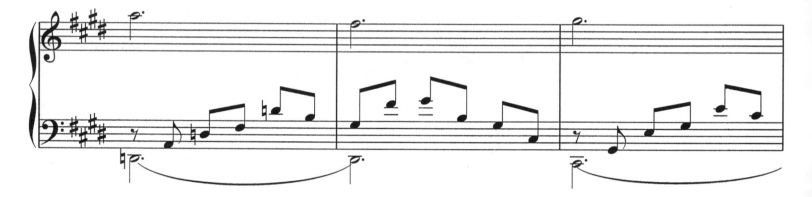

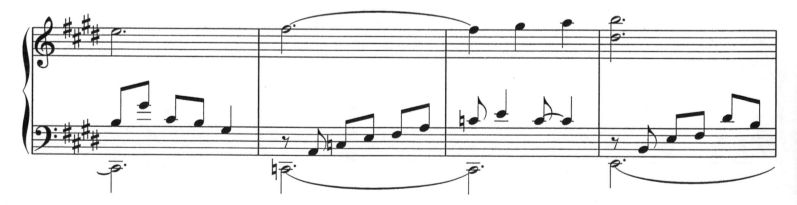

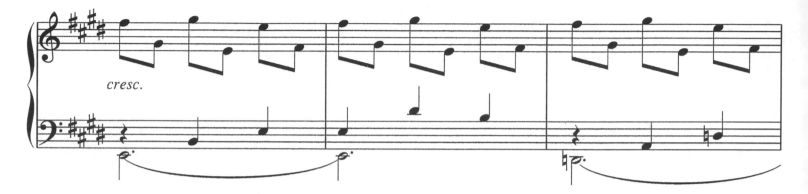

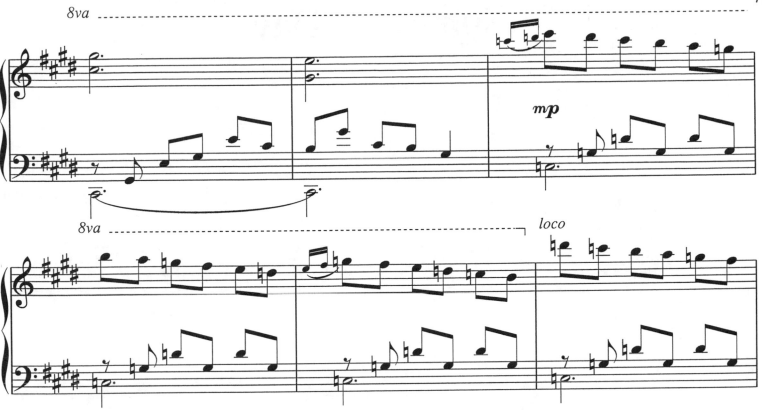

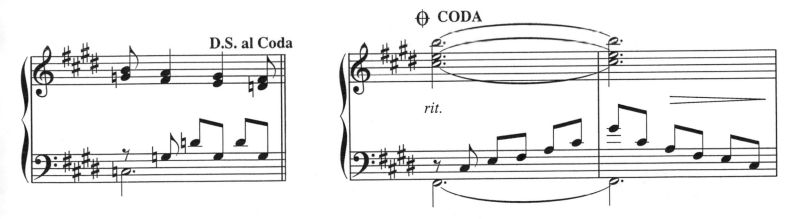

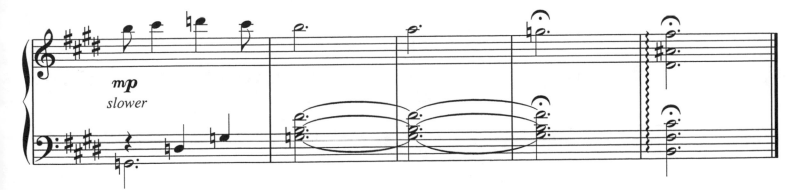

Summer's Day

By SUZANNE CIANI

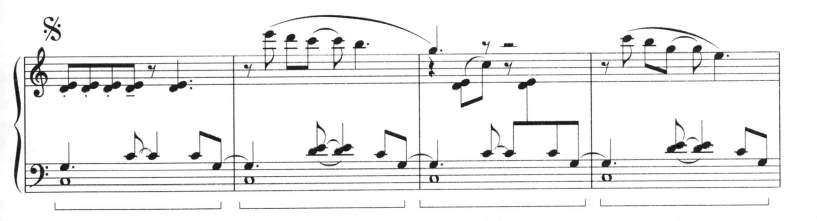

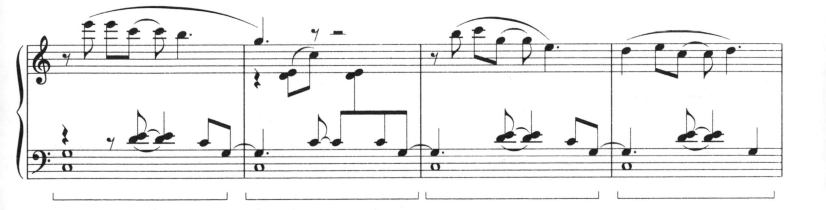

sim.

To Coda ⊕

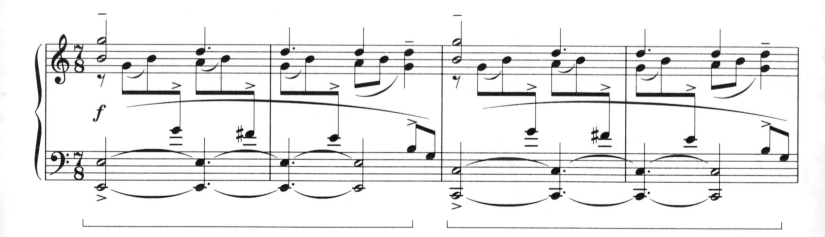

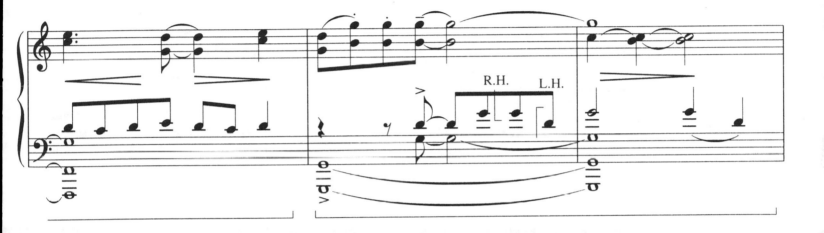

D.S. al Coda

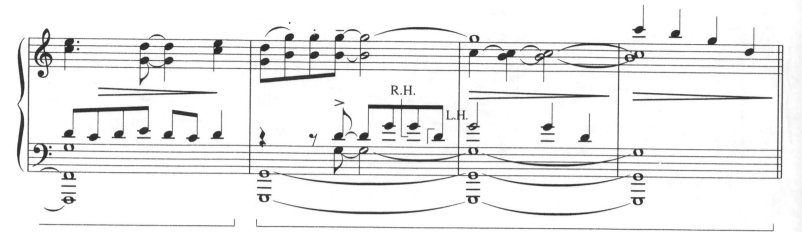

⊕ *Coda*

Improvise freely to end

The Velocity of Love

By SUZANNE CIANI

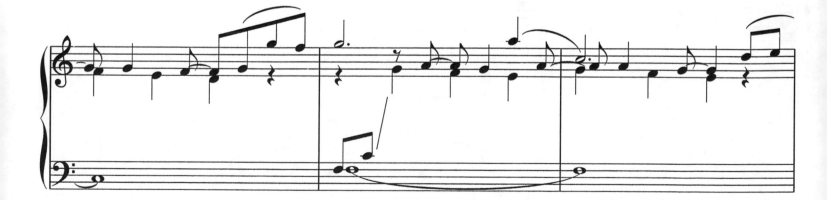

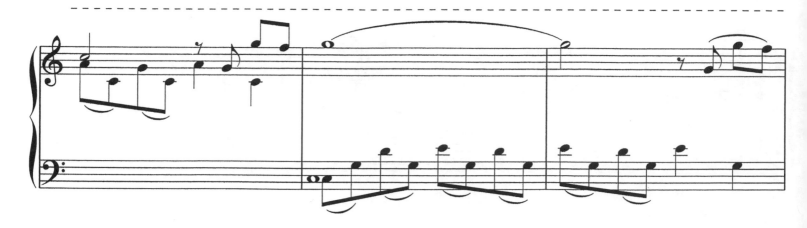

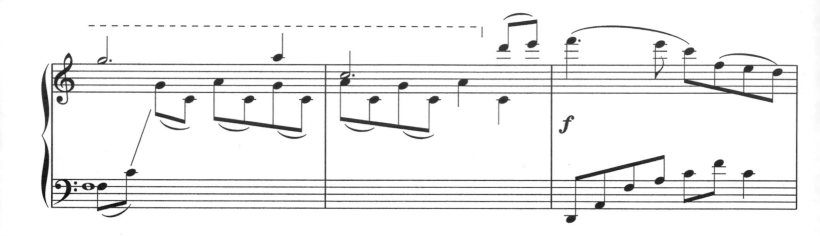

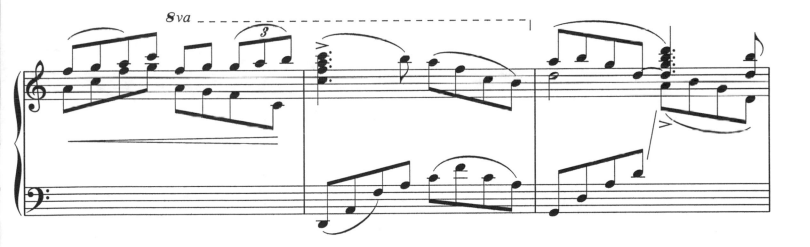

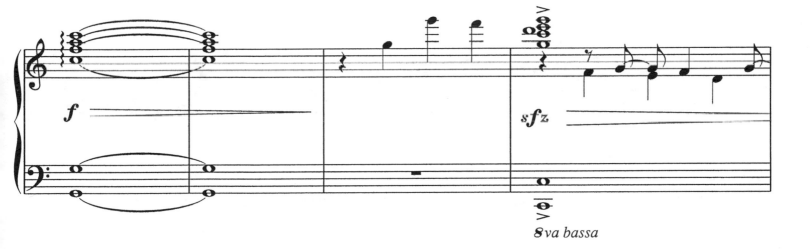

8va bassa

fading away

Wedding Rain

By LIZ STORY

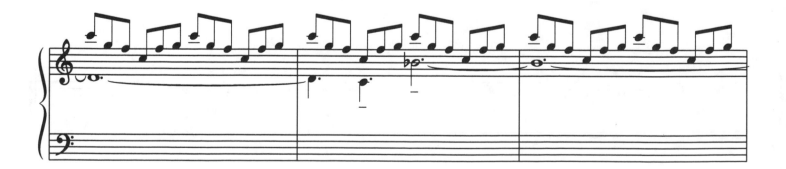

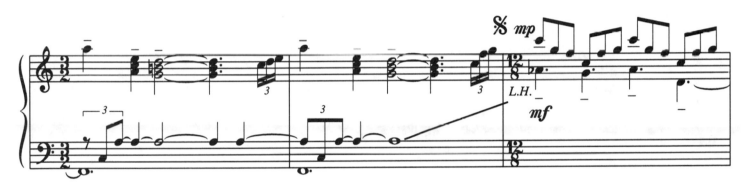

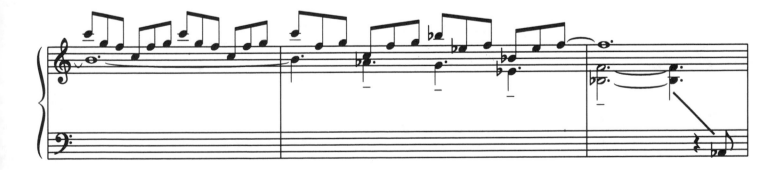

4th time to Coda III ⊕

2nd time to Coda I;
3rd time to Coda II ⊕

espressivo

D.S. al Coda I

CODA I

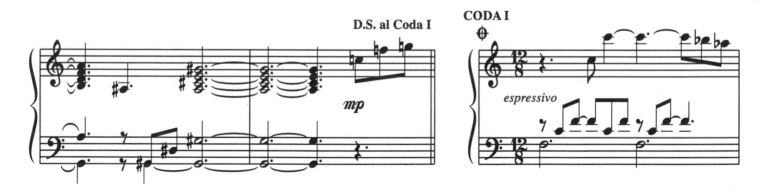

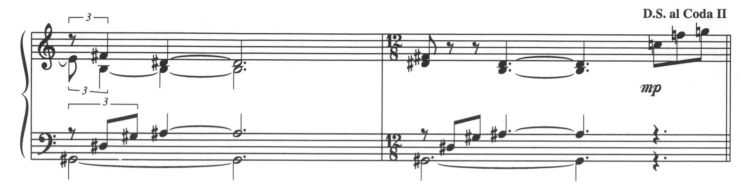

D.S. al Coda II

CODA II

CODA III

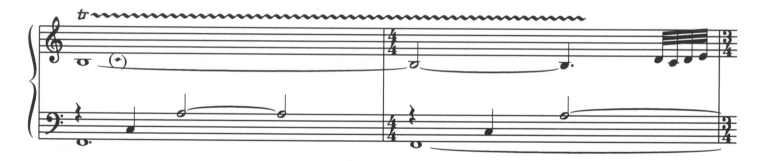